THE BRIDGE FROM A-Z

Linking PEI & NB, Canada

Written by: Kathy Creaghan Gray

Illustrated by: Elizabeth Scott

Story Editor: Sheree Fitch

Printed in Prince Edward Island by Williams and Crue (1982) Ltd.
Published by Quality Action Consulting

Text and Illustrations © 1996 by Quality Action Consulting

ISBN 0-9680554-0-0

The Bridge From A-Z takes a novel look at the bridge connecting Prince Edward Island to New Brunswick. This bridge shows how the Maritimes are at the cutting edge of modern technology.

Williams and Crue, the Island's largest printer, has invested in modern equipment to provide our clients in the region with state of the art printing methods.

We offer complete printing services from design consultation to high resolution scanning and printing. **The Bridge From A-Z** was produced totally in house.

We are proud to have been chosen to produce this book.

Williams & Crue (1982) Ltd.
4 Queen Street • Summerside • Prince Edward Island • Canada • C1N 4K5
Telephone 902-436-2125 • Fax 902-436-3027

We would like to thank

Strait Crossing Development Inc. for information content,

Brian Gray for artwork design and Sheree Fitch for her

continuous input and expertise as our editor.

This book is dedicated to our children,

David, Kari, Kelly and Willie.

We're going to cross the bridge
We're going to cross the bridge
We're going to the Island
We're going to cross the bridge

Follow me, I'll show you more
I'll show you more, I'll show you more
Follow me, I'll show you more
I'll show you how we linked the shores

ARE YOU READY?
ARE YOU SET?
LET'S GO THROUGH THE ALPHABET!

*This verse may be sung to the tune of "Farmer in the Dell".

Approach Bridges

The Northumberland Strait Bridge is really three bridges joined together, two inshore approach bridges and a main bridge in deep water. New Brunswick's approach bridge is twice as long as Prince Edward Island's because the water on the New Brunswick side is not as deep.

Barge

There are lots of barges in the Northumberland Strait. My favorite, "Betty L" crane barge digs and puts in place hardpoint positioning pads for each pier. "Buzzard" Jack-up barge takes over after a base is placed and seals it to the foundation.

Cranes

There are more than 50 cranes in the PEI Staging Facility! A floating crane called the "Svanen" puts the main bridge parts in place. It is three times the height of the Charlottetown Prince Edward Hotel and can lift 1000 rhinoceroses, 600 hippopotamuses, 500 elephants, 100 gorillas, 50 lions and a blue whale (8200 tonnes), all at the same time!

Design

The thirteen kilometer bridge is designed like the arched back of a kitten. Boats go under the belly of the kitten, the navigation span. This unique bridge is designed to last for one hundred years.

Environment

The environment and all wildlife in the surrounding area are protected. Nesting platforms were built for the osprey, an endangered bird found in the Cape Jourimain National Wildlife area.

Foundations

Like stepping stones for a giant, rock foundations cross the bottom of the Northumberland Strait. These foundations support the piers and make the bridge secure.

Girders
Girders are the bridge deck that cars, buses, jeeps, trucks and motor bikes drive across. A girder sits on top of each pier shaft.

Heavy Transport Vehicles

The Huisman heavy transport vehicles are called sledges and were named the lobster and the turtle. They carried the main bridge pieces in the PEI Staging Facility and to the jetty in the Northumberland Strait.

Ice

The Northumberland Strait Bridge is the longest bridge in the world over ice-covered water. Bridge piers have specially designed ice shields to protect the bridge from ice forces and help the natural flow of ice in the Strait.

Jourimain Island

On the New Brunswick side, the bridge begins at Jourimain Island. The surrounding area, Cape Jourimain, is one of forty-five designated wildlife areas in Canada.

Keys

Shear keys are drilled into a rock foundation to secure approach bridge piers. Four of the approach bridge piers used a steel enclosure called a cofferdam to provide a dry environment for workers to install shear keys. The other bridge piers did not need to use a cofferdam.

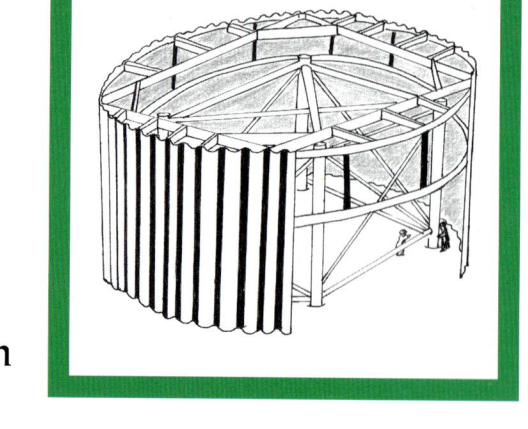

Launching Truss

The launching truss places bridge pieces together to make up the approach bridges. This truss is constructed from steel, built in many triangles, giving it the strength needed to lift heavy bridge pieces.

Machines

Machines are used on and off the construction site for many different jobs. Men and women must be specially trained before operating any machinery.

Northumberland Strait

The Northumberland Strait separates Prince Edward Island from New Brunswick and Nova Scotia. From early settlement throughout the 1800's, the ice boat was the only way people and mail could get across the Strait in the winter.

Open

In the late 1800's, ferries provided year round transportation to and from Prince Edward Island. From 1997 onwards, the Northumberland Strait Bridge will provide year round transportation and will remain open to the public twenty-four hours a day, seven days a week.

Piers

If you counted every pier on the Northumberland Strait Bridge, it would add up to a total of sixty-five. The main bridge has forty-four piers, New Brunswick's approach bridge has fourteen and Prince Edward Island's has seven.

Quality

Teams of people work together, check their work, then have it checked by someone else to make sure that the job is done right and the highest quality of materials and services are used.

Recreation

Recreation is a great way to escape from everyday work and provides a good form of exercise. New Brunswick and Prince Edward Island offer many areas designed especially for fun and recreation.

Service

Twenty-four hour bridge services, including maintenance and operation, are provided. A shuttle bus service is used to take pedestrians and cyclists across the bridge.

Toll

A toll is money you pay to cross the bridge. Tolls are collected on the Prince Edward Island side of the bridge in Borden-Carleton. No tolls are collected on the New Brunswick side of the bridge.

Union

A union is an organized group of workers. With over two thousand people working to build the bridge, many different trade unions were represented throughout the project.

Vessels

Throughout construction of the bridge, dozens of support vessels, tugs, crewboats, material barges & scows, and spud barges were used by Strait Crossing.

Width

The Northumberland Strait Bridge is the same width as a two lane highway, with emergency shoulders on each side. Guardrail to guardrail, that's almost double what a full-grown kangaroo can jump!

X

X marks the spot where Strait Crossing's construction workers placed the first main bridge girder, pier three, on October 1st, 1995. Crossing the Northumberland Strait Bridge is history in the making!

ard

Approach bridge pieces were built at the fabrication yard in Bayfield, New Brunswick. Main bridge pieces were built at the yard in Borden-Carleton, Prince Edward Island.

Zipper

To be safe, workers must zipper up their life jackets when they are anywhere near water. On land, eye and ear protection, proper footwear, a hard hat and flourescent vest must be worn at all times.

We went across the bridge
We went across the bridge
We went to the Island
We went across the bridge

You followed me, I showed you more
I showed you more, I showed you more
You followed me, I showed you more
I showed you how we linked the shores

YOU WERE READY!
YOU WERE SET!
WE ZIPPED RIGHT THROUGH THE ALPHABET!!

See you on the other side...

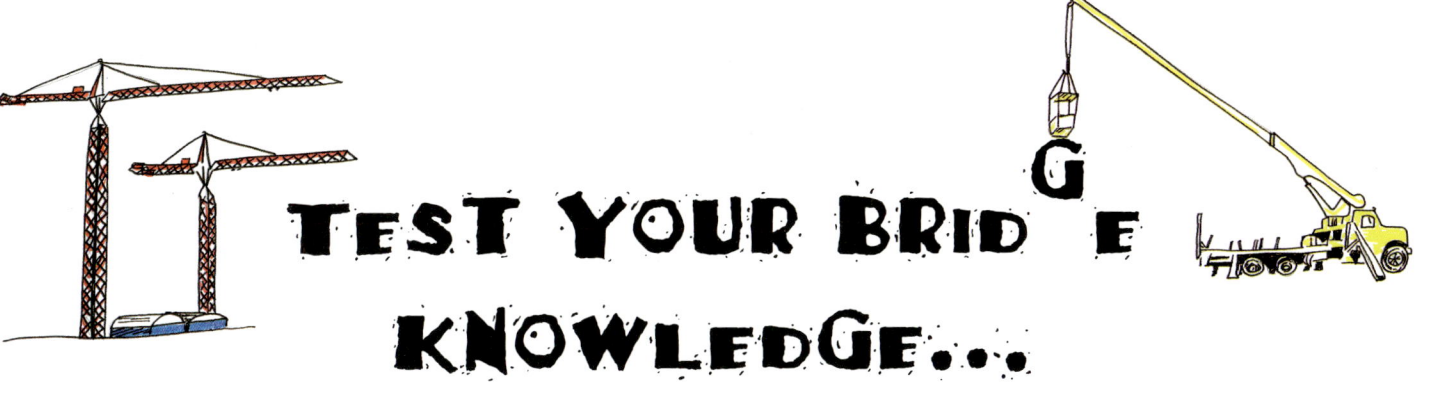

TEST YOUR BRIDGE KNOWLEDGE...

1. How many bridges are joined together to make up the Northumberland Strait Bridge?

2. What is the name of the floating crane that can lift up to 8200 tonnes?

3. What is the navigation span used for?

4. What are the names of the two Huisman sledges used to carry main bridge pieces?

5. In New Brunswick, where does the bridge begin?

6. Where does the bridge begin in Prince Edward Island?

7. What is the name of the water that separates PEI from NB and NS?

8. If you counted every pier on the bridge, what would be the total number?

9. How do pedestrians and cyclists cross the bridge?

10. How many years is the bridge designed to last?

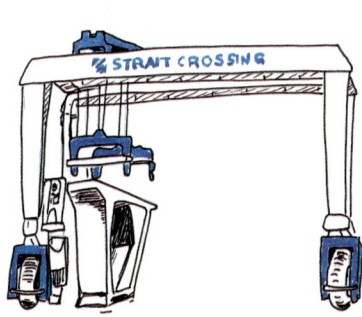

ANSWERS
1. three
2. Svanen
3. large boats to pass under the bridge
4. Turtle/Lobster
5. Jourimain Island
6. Borden-Carleton
7. Northumberland Strait
8. sixty-five
9. shuttle bus
10. one hundred

THE NORTHUMBERLAND STRAIT BRIDGE PROJECT

Developers:
Strait Crossing/ The Strait Crossing team have designed and built thousands of bridges around the world.

History:
Under the terms of Prince Edward Island's entry into Confederation in 1873, the Government of Canada is obligated to provide year round transportation to and from Prince Edward Island. Over the years, various proposals have been considered for fixed crossings ranging from a tunnel in the late 1800s to a combined causeway, tunnel and bridge in the 1960s.

In 1987, the Government of Canada issued a proposal call challenging the private sector to devise an environmentally, technically, and financially sound alternative to the ferry system. Strait Crossing devised a competitive financial solution that assumes responsibility for 100% of all costs of construction, operation and maintenance until 2032, after which time ownership of the bridge will be transferred to the government.

Environment:
The Environmental Management Plan is based on hundreds of studies and covers the pre-construction, construction and operational phases of the project. An Environmental Protection Plan has been designed to ensure that prevention of any potential adverse effects of construction on the the marine, terrestrial and socio-economic environments is carefully considered and mitigated. To detect changes caused by interaction of the project with the environment, Environmental Monitoring Effects Programs have been established. Environmental Enhancement Programs such as nesting platforms for osprey, establishing new habitat, planting trees and agreements with conservation groups to enhance existing wetlands have also been established.

Bridge Design:
The bridge crosses the Northumberland Strait between Jourimain Island, New Brunswick and Borden-Carleton, Prince Edward Island, the narrowest point between the two provinces.

The 12.9 km structure will be completed in 1997 and, upon completion, will carry two lanes of traffic. Guardrail to guardrail, the bridge is 11 m wide, including one lane and one emergency shoulder in each direction. Bridge design and construction methods are based on proven technology.

The typical elevation is 40 m off the water; typical clearance, 28 m off the water x 220 m wide. The navigation span elevation is 60 m off the water; navigation clearance 49 m off the water x 200 m wide.

The installation of each main bridge component requires one day to complete. There are 175 main bridge components.

Approach Bridge:
PEI Approach Bridge: 7 spans, 580 m in total
NB Approach Bridge: 14 spans, 1300 m in total
Foundation: pile cap/ice shield on drilled shear keys or piles
Piers: rectangular hollow shafts
Spans: length; 93 m

Main Bridge:
Footings: gravity based founded on bedrock
Piers: octagonal hollow shafts
Girders: precast concrete box girders, ranging 4.5-14 m deep
Spans - 11,000 m total; 250 m / typical span

Vessels:
Strait Crossings vessels, the Betty L, the Buzzard Jack-up Barge and the HLV Svanen work simultaneously in the Northumberland Strait to install main bridge components.

Betty L, crane barge, excavates and positions the hard points for each pier.
The Buzzard jackup barge concretes the pier bases to the prepared foundation.

The Svanen is a twin-hulled floating crane with a lifting capability of 8200 tonnes. This unique vessel is 99 m long, 72 m wide and 100 m high. The Svanen places a pier shaft and a main girder individually on each pier base. A drop-in span is then put in place to complete the span.